# Supply and Demand

by Jamie A. Schroeder

## Table of Contents

What Are Needs? What Are Wants? . . . . . . . . . . . . . . . . . 4

What Is Supply? What Is Demand? . . . . . . . . . . . . . . . . 10

Why Do Some Things Cost More? . . . . . . . . . . . . . . . . . 14

Glossary and Index . . . . . . . . . . . . . . . . . . . . . . . . . . . . 20

# I need to know these words.

**bicycle**

**shoes**

**skateboard**

**store**

**sweater**

**video game**

# What Are Needs? What Are Wants?

What are **needs**? A family goes to a store. The family buys food. Food is a need.

▲ This family buys food at a store.

Water is a need, too. People cannot live without water. Things people cannot live without are needs.

▲ People must drink water every day.

Do you wear shoes? Most people wear shoes. Some shoes are a need. John must buy shoes.

▲ These shoes are a need.

Mia buys a CD. Is a CD a need? A CD is a **want**. Things people can live without are wants.

▲ A CD is not a need.

Jim buys this guitar. Mike buys this video game. Are these things needs or wants?

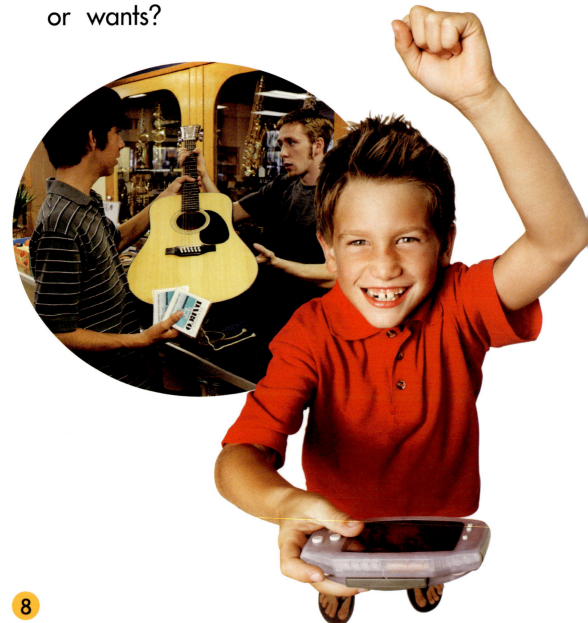

What types of things are needs?
What types of things are wants?

| Needs | Wants |
|---|---|
|  |  |

▲ Can you add more things to these charts?

# What Is Supply? What Is Demand?

This store has a large **supply** of bicycles. Many people buy the bicycles. Many people like bicycles.

▲ This store has many bicycles.

The **demand** is high for bicycles. The demand is high when many people buy something.

▲ These people have bicycles.

The store also has skateboards.
The store does not sell many skateboards.
The demand for skateboards is low.

▲ This boy does not sell many skateboards.

The store has many skateboards. The supply of skateboards is high. The supply is high when few people buy something.

▲ The store has a large supply of skateboards.

## Why Do Some Things Cost More?

Look at this sweater. The sweater comes from a **factory**. The machines in the factory make many sweaters every day.

▲ This machine makes sweaters.

This store always has many sweaters. The supply is high. The cost is low because the supply is high.

▲ The store always has a large supply of these sweaters.

This woman makes sweaters. The woman can make only a few sweaters every week. The supply is low.

▲ This woman makes sweaters by hand.

Many people want these sweaters. Few sweaters are for sale at one time. The supply is low. The **price** of the sweaters is high.

▲ There are a few sweaters.
   The cost of these sweaters is high.

Most needs cost more when demand is high. Most wants cost more when demand is high, too.

Look at the chart. Which affects price more, supply or demand?

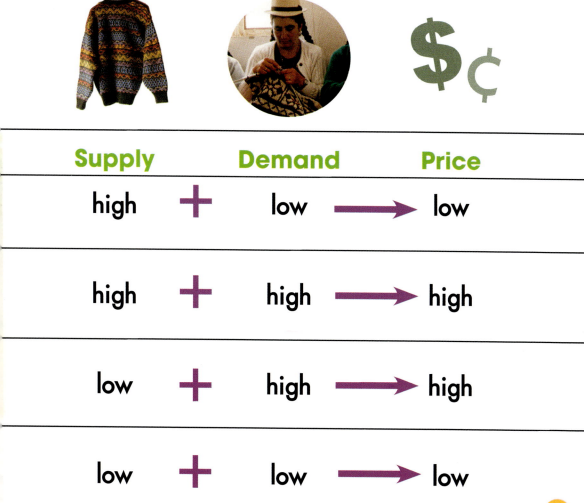

| Supply | | Demand | | Price |
|---|---|---|---|---|
| high | + | low | → | low |
| high | + | high | → | high |
| low | + | high | → | high |
| low | + | low | → | low |

# Glossary

**demand (dih-MAND):** the need for something
See page 11.

**factory (FAK-tuh-ree):** building where people make things
See page 14.

**need (NEED):** something living things cannot survive without
See page 4.

**price (PRISE):** the cost of something
See page 17.

**supply (suh-PLY):** an amount of something
See page 10.

**want (WANT):** things people can live without
See page 7.

# Index

demand, 11–12, 18–19
factory, 14
need, 4–7, 9, 18

price, 17, 19
supply, 10, 13, 15–17, 19
want, 7–9, 18